Hello, My Name is Louisiana Purchase O'Leary!

by
Jonathan M. Hickman

Illustrated by
Paul Dillon

Dedicated to
My beautiful wife Carla,
My adventurous son Daniel,
And my courageous daughter Rachel.

Forest Park
History Museum
Muny
Art Museum
Pavilion
Science Center

Have you ever wondered how you got your name?

Maybe you are named after one of your parents or grandparents.
Perhaps you are named for an aunt or uncle in your family.

Some people are named after characters from a book, play or
movie. In some cases, parents have named children after a name
they have always liked.

Whatever the reason, your name is no accident. Your name has
a history.

LOUISIANA
PURCHASE
1804
Thomas Jefferson

In the year 1902, the city of St. Louis, Missouri was busy preparing to be the site of the 1904 World's Fair. People from around the world were going to be coming to St. Louis to celebrate the 100th anniversary of the Louisiana Purchase.

President Thomas Jefferson purchased the Louisiana Territory in 1804, doubling the size of the United States.

Many people were needed to design and build the buildings that would be used during the fair. And it would all take place in a large park in St. Louis named Forest Park.

One of the construction workers at the fair was a man named Lawrence O'Leary. He and his wife Mary lived in a worker's tent in Forest Park while they both worked on the construction of the upcoming fair.

Richard?
Ethan?
Michael?
Peter?
Phillip?
Robert?
Charles?
Sammuel?
David?
James?
Sarah?
Rebecca?
Carol?
Elaine?
Helen?
Anna?
Irma?
Lucy?
Amy?
Frances?

Lawrence and Mary learned that they were going to have a baby. They were both very excited. They had never been parents before and they didn't know if they were going to have a baby boy or girl.

What would they name their new son or daughter? There were so many different names to consider. Lawrence and Mary decided to name their son or daughter a name that no one had ever considered.

Birth Certificate
This is to Certify that
Louisiana Purchase O'Leary
Was Born on August 20, 1902
To Mary and Lawrence O'Leary

On August 20, 1902, the O'Learys had a baby girl. It was the first baby born on what would be the Louisiana Purchase Exhibition. The O'Learys named their daughter Louisiana Purchase O'Leary.

At first, Louisiana Purchase and her parents made their home in the tent they had been using. Stories in the local newspapers told about the baby girl with the unusual name living in a tent in the park.

Many people came to the O'Leary's tent to visit the young family. Several visitors gave the family money or baby gifts.

WORLD'S FAIR BABY CHRISTENED

Louisiana Purchase O'Leary officially christened at
Louisiana Purchase Exposition Administration Building

On September 6th, Lawrence, Mary, and their baby met with local church ministers at the Administration Building of the Fair. They officially christened their daughter Louisiana Purchase O'Leary. Hundreds of people came to see the event.

The local newspapers that wrote about the event nicknamed her, "The World's Fair Baby."

Following the news stories, a doll was created and fashioned after Louisiana Purchase O'Leary. It came with doll clothes reminiscent of the 1904 era. The doll kits had little silver cups similar to the ones used at her christening.

Louisiana Purchase O'Leary

As Louisiana Purchase grew she was enrolled in local schools in
St. Louis. The teachers in the schools would try to shorten her name.
They would call her Louise. Some of her classmates tried to nickname
her "Lou." But she would have none of it. She would correct both
her teachers and classmates and tell them, "My name is Louisiana
Purchase. I like my name very much, please call me by my name!"

Mueller's Emporium

Louisiana Purchase continued her education and later worked at various jobs after her schooling. When she met new people she would introduce herself by saying, "Hello, my name is Louisiana Purchase O'Leary." People would respond, "You've got to be kidding!" She would enjoy the surprise of people's reactions. But more importantly, it gave her the chance to tell new aquaintances how she got her name and the story behind it.

1904 St. Louis
World's Fair

The Louisiana Purchase Exposition, better known as the 1904 St. Louis World's Fair, became one of the most famous world fairs of all time. People traveled to St. Louis from all over the country and the world to see the lights, exhibits, music and food. Famous movies and songs have been written about the fair.

25

But before all of the amazing sights and sounds of this memorable fair, there was the story of a little girl... a little girl named Louisiana Purchase O'Leary. Louisiana Purchase O'Leary loved her name, and she loved the history of her name.

The End

About the Author

Jonathan Hickman graduated from the University of Missouri with a degree in elementary education. While as a student and later as a teacher, he developed a love for children's literature and storytelling. This is his first published story.

About the Illustrator

Paul Dillon is a graduate of the University of Arkansas at Little Rock and an accomplished cartoonist/illustrator whose work has appeared in numerous children's story and activity books, and in a variety of periodicals.

Afterword:

Louisiana Purchase O'Leary was indeed a real person. She was born on August 20, 1902 and died on June 18, 2003. She was born, and as an infant, lived in a tent in what is today Forest Park, in St. Louis City. Later in life she married a man named Harry Wampler and went by the name Louisiana Purchase Wampler. She is buried in St. Matthew Cemetery in St. Louis City.

Printed in the USA
CPSIA information can be obtained
at www.ICGtesting.com
LVHW061056030324

773143LV00037BA/47